IMAGES
of England

BICESTER
AND CHESTERTON

19.

07.

20.

2. D.

11.

21.

Bicester postcard from the 1960s. Top left is the Old Post Office in Sheep Street, now the Penny Black public house. Bottom left is 'Captain's Walk', a local name for this path by the wall of Bicester House which was once the home of Captain Fane. The centre and bottom right scenes remain unchanged today. The large block of buildings behind the cars in the top right scene was demolished in 1963 to ease traffic congestion.

IMAGES
of England

BICESTER
AND CHESTERTON

Compiled by
Bicester Local History Society

TEMPUS

First published 1999
Copyright © Bicester Local History Society, 1999

Tempus Publishing Limited
The Mill, Brimscombe Port,
Stroud, Gloucestershire, GL5 2QG

ISBN 0 7524 1699 5

Typesetting and origination by
Tempus Publishing Limited
Printed in Great Britain by
Midway Clark Printing, Wiltshire

Contents

A mile and a quarter south of present-day Bicester, at the crossing of two major Roman roads, lies the earth works of the Roman settlement of Alchester. The settlement was of major importance to the occupying Romans.

Acknowledgements

We are very grateful for the loan of photographs from Don Blee, Mary Brydon, Connie Harris, Frances Harris, Peter Judd, Dave Powell, John Roberts, Megan Savins, Bert Simons, and local photographer Michael Morgan.

Picture Post photographs by kind permission of the Hulton Getty Picture Collection.

This book was compiled by the Bicester Local History Society under the editorial supervision of Sally James, Ruth Martin, Gerry Mason, John Roberts, Mick Wall and Wendy Wall.

Thanks go to the many individuals who supplied information for the captions. Without their knowledge of local people and events, the book would not have been possible.

Introduction

If you are anything like me, you have already looked through the pictures and read the captions, and now visit the introduction to see what the book is all about. Hopefully, it requires no explanation. The beauty of a book of photographs is that it stands on its own without an overlong narrative.

The idea for a book of photographs came to me many years ago. On first suggestion to the History Society it appeared to be a very daunting task because we had few photographs of our own from which to draw. Unlike other towns, Bicester seems to have been largely avoided by photographers producing postcard scenes in any quantities. We are fortunate, though, to have had the Morgan family of photographers who have produced a good photographic archive of scenes and events. Michael Morgan is still recording local scenes today for posterity. A number of smaller collections are also held by individuals with family history in the town, and we are grateful to them all for allowing us to use their photographs in this book.

The village of Chesterton, which lies just over a mile south-west of Bicester, is also featured. The photographs of Chesterton were a real find, having been rescued from a bonfire after a house clearance in the town. They paint a fascinating picture of village life in the latter part of the nineteenth century. The photographs were presented in an album, and the majority was accompanied by a handwritten caption detailing the place, date and time of taking. The care taken is remarkable and of great value to the local historian. They are included in the book along with the accompanying caption because it was too good an opportunity to miss.

Historically, the town of Bicester has led a largely uneventful life. There is a debate about the origin of the name for the town. The Doomsday Book of 1086 records the town as *Berncester*. In 1793 the name for the town was given as *Burcester*, and the present day spelling of *Bicester* became standard in the nineteenth century.

The town developed in two parts, King's End and Market End. Tradition has it that the settlement of King's End was founded by Birinus, seventh century Bishop of Dorchester, and subsequently destroyed by the Danes around 912. The nuns of Markyate, Bedfordshire, obtained land at the beginning of the thirteenth century and their cottages and tenants constituted most of the settlement. By 1316 the Manor was known as King's End and in 1377 a licence to allow a three-day annual trade fair was granted. Markyate Priory was suppressed in 1536 and in 1542 what was called 'the Manor of the nuns place in Bicester King's End' was sold into private ownership. In 1584 the Manor was conveyed to the Coker family and Bicester House remained in their ownership for nearly four centuries.

Adjacent and to the east, the settlement of Market End (or Bury End) developed. The Lord of the Manor was Gilbert Bassett who, in 1182, gave land to the Augustians to found a priory on land to the west of the River Bure (today's Old Place Yard). The Priory was dissolved in 1536; ten years after King Henry VIII had visited it. In 1239 a charter was granted to William de Longspee to hold a weekly market; in 1252 licence was given to hold a fair for three days on and around the feast of St Edburg on the 18 July; in 1441 Robert Brooke was granted a Friday market which possibly included a livestock market. The markets sustained a community larger than an ordinary agrarian village, and leases of houses suggest a prosperous merchant community in the thirteenth century. Two-storey houses with cellars and solars (withdrawing rooms) were built continuously on long narrow burgage plots along Market End and Causeway. Although these were replaced in the sixteenth and seventeenth centuries, the mediaeval town plan can still be identified.

The two townships shared St Edburg's Parish Church. The importance of the church is evidenced by the formation of the Bicester Deanery comprising thirty-three churches before the end of the twelfth century. The existing church still incorporates some late Saxon work, but most of it dates from the twelfth to fifteenth centuries.

The fourteenth and fifteenth centuries saw economic decline exacerbated by the Black Death in 1349, floods in 1412, and poor harvests. The sixteenth and seventeenth centuries were prosperous times and the town saw much rebuilding including the use of stone from the dissolved Priory. Sheep Street developed at this time when the livestock market outgrew the Market Square. Burgage plots extended from Causeway, northwards either side of Sheep Street, and the present day town centre was formed. As Market End became more prosperous and commercial, so King's End remained quietly rural. In fact, two farms remained working well into the middle of the twentieth century. Bicester continued to comprise two townships until the Urban District Council was created in 1894.

Much change has taken place during the twentieth century. The arrival of RAF Bicester in 1916 and COD Bicester in 1942 made new house building a necessity, and many new estates have been created since the 1930s. More recently, the arrival of the M40 and good rail links have made the town and surrounding area a very attractive location for the commuter. New industry and business also makes its demands on local housing needs. Like many other towns, new housing and new people seem to arrive daily and a town with a population of 3,110 in 1939 will have well over 25,000 inhabitants by the start of the new Millennium.

I hope that old and new residents alike will enjoy looking at this book and that visitors will gain pleasure from seeing the town as it was. It is worth taking time to see that, in spite of its growth, the town is not so very different today. In compiling this book we have attempted to give an insight into the life of Bicester and its people over the last 100 years or so. We have included historical information in the captions, which we hope will enhance your enjoyment of the book.

Gerry Mason
Chairman, Bicester Local History Society.

Mrs W. J. French on 7 August 1921 celebrating her birthday at the age of 101. It is interesting to note that during her life she witnessed no less than five monarchs on the throne. Notice the abundance of intricate lace work in this picture.

One
King's End

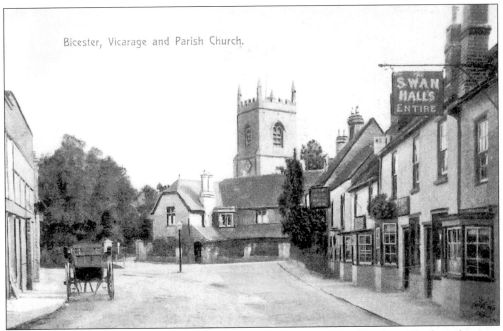

Church Street, c. 1900. The building on the far-left is Hollis wheelwrights. The horseless cart at the side of the road is probably awaiting repair.

Oxford Road looking north, c. 1930. The old entrance to Bicester House can be seen in the distance. The row of thatched cottages on the left was demolished in January 1958 at a cost of £238, producing 300 tons of building stone. Behind the wall on the right is the cottage hospital built in 1908 for £1,100.

A scene published in the *Picture Post* in 1950, 'on the way to morning school'. A young boy leads blind Frank Wilkins along the Oxford Road on their way to Sunday school at the local Methodist church.

King's End, *c.* 1900. Looking north to the old gateway to Bicester House which was relocated round the corner opposite Coker Close when the road was extended to Field Street. The signs for the Fox Inn and Parrott's coachbuilders can be seen on the left and for Stockley's carpenters on the right. The entrance to Piggy Lane can be seen on the right in front of the three-storied house, South View. This is the main road into the town from Oxford.

Cripps coachbuilders, c. 1910. Stockley's carpenters has been replaced but the same type of work continues. The Oxfordshire wagon awaiting repair belongs to Isaac Jakeman of Chesterton. Note the coachbuilders in their bowler hats.

Carnival float, July 1932. The occasion is unknown, but the float won second prize. Here it can be seen on the Oxford Road passing the hospital wall and Piggy Lane.

Sheep Fair in King's End, 5 August 1909. Behind the trees to the left is Bicester House. The house on the extreme right was the home of Mrs Rashleigh in the 1930s. She was a keen hunter and had stables at the rear of the property. After the Second World War, Miss Johnson ran a prep school in the building.

The Sheep Fair in progress further up King's End. Manor Farm with its porch can be seen between the trees. The tree (centre-right) was a favourite spot for the Salvation Army Band to play and it became known as the Hallelujah Tree. Notice the different types of hat worn by the men and that they are all wearing one.

The Six Bells decorated for Queen Victoria's Jubilee in 1897. On the right is Mr W. E. Smith outside his bakery. Mr Smith's grandson is the present owner of the building, now a private house.

Nos. 9 and 11 Church Street. Render covers up a date stone on the property. Uncovered today, it reveals that the building dates from 1676. Outside the door is Mr W. E. Smith who operated a bakery and confectionery business from the premises. Notice the glass bottles of sweets in the window.

This postcard, date-stamped 11 September 1909, clearly shows the vicarage in front of the church. The building to the right of it was the Blue Coat School. The message on the card reads: 'Dear B. I am sorry to say I shall not be able to come on Saturday as we have not finished cutting the wheat the weather is so hindering. I expect you are getting on with your harvest. Hope you will enjoy yourself at W Feast Monday. Love to all from all. W F'. 'W Feast' referred to the annual fair held in the town of Witney.

THE BICESTER NATIONAL SCHOOLS.

Bicester National School was built in 1859. These pictures formed the front page of a leaflet produced to advertise a fundraising event for the enlargement and improvement of the school.

A Grand Fancy Bazaar

AND

SALE OF WORK,

In aid of the Fund for the Enlargement and Improvement of the above Schools, will be held in

ST. EDBURG'S HALL, BICESTER,

ON WEDNESDAY & THURSDAY THE 13TH & 14TH APRIL, 1898.

HER GRACE THE

DUCHESS OF MARLBOROUGH

Has kindly consented to OPEN the Bazaar on the First Day (Wednesday).

THE EARL AND COUNTESS OF JERSEY,
THE EARL OF COTTENHAM,
THE VISCOUNT VALENTIA, M.P.,
THE LORD SAYE AND SELE,
THE LORD BISHOP OF READING,
LIEUT.-COLONEL GOSLING,

THE REV. W. H. DRAPER,
G. H. MORRELL, ESQ., M.P., AND MRS. MORRELL,
E. SLATER-HARRISON, ESQ.,
LADY PEYTON,
MRS. HOARE, AND MRS. TUBB.

STALLHOLDERS.

Stall 1—(Fancy Articles)—THE LADY MARGARET VILLIERS, THE LADY MARY VILLIERS, AND MRS. R. D'OYLY THOMAS.
,, 2—(Cushions and Pincushions)—THE HON. MRS. CRAWFURD AND MRS. FANE.
,, 3—(General Articles, supplied by School Children and others)—MISS BROOKE AND MISS DANIELL.
,, 4—(Fancy Articles, Pictures, China, &c.—MRS. DRINKWATER AND MISS DEWAR.
,, 5—(Books and Music) MISS E. FLEMONS.
,, 6—(Fancy Articles)—MRS. HENDRIKS, MRS. J. F. JONES, MRS. KYNASTON, MISS ELLEN JONES.
,, 7—(Flowers)—MRS. WALSH.
,, 8—(Farm Produce)—MRS. AUGER AND MRS. FINCH.
,, 9—(Cakes)—MRS. BOUGHTON AND MISS COLEMAN.
,, 10—(Sweets)—MISS KATIE FINCH.

Towards the Furnishing of these Stalls any Contributions in Money or Kind will be thankfully accepted.

☞ THE REFRESHMENTS will be under the superintendence of MRS. GOBLE, MRS. COOKE, and MRS. C. A. KING.

These two pictures formed the back page of the advertising leaflet. The school is now called St Edburg's School and is situated behind the church.

. . Various Entertainments . .

✦ ✦ ✦

ARE being organised to take place at intervals during the time the Bazaar is open, amongst which will be a **Washing Competition** (Prizes given by the makers of Sunlight Soap), **Humorous Sketches** by Messrs. H. W. and P. J. Bayzand, &c., &c., the whole to conclude with

A DRAMATIC PERFORMANCE

In the Corn Exchange,

BY MEMBERS OF THE OXFORD CITY DRAMATIC SOCIETY.

The whole of the arrangements are under the personal supervision of the following Committee:—

MRS. AUGER.	MR. T. C. FINCH,	MRS. KYNASTON,
MRS. BOUGHTON,	MRS. FINCH,	MR. J. B. LAYTON,
MR. C. W. BRABANT,	MISS KATIE FINCH,	REV. C. PAGE,
MISS BRABANT,	MISS E. FLEMONS,	MR. W. H. PIGGOTT,
MISS BROOKE,	MRS. GOBLE,	MR. T. G. PRENTICE.
MISS COLEMAN,	MR. T. GRIMSLEY (Sheep Street),	MRS. SCRIVENER,
MRS COOKE,	MR. J. W. HUNT,	MISS SHILLINGFORD,
HON. MRS. CRAWFURD,	MRS. HUNT,	MISS H. SHILLINGFORD,
MISS DANIELL,	MRS. HENDRIKS,	MRS. THOMAS,
MR. W. DRINKWATER.	MR. H. C. JAGGER,	MR. H. TUBB,
MRS. DRINKWATER,	MRS. J. F. JONES,	MR. G. WALSH,
MRS. FANE,	MRS. C. A. KING,	MRS. WALSH.

Chairman—**Rev. G. P. Crawfurd** (Vicar).　　　*Secretary*—**Mr. J. F. Jones.**

St Edburg's Church dates from the twelfth century. It stands outside the boundary of the earlier Bicester Priory which had its own church. The priory church disappeared at the time of the dissolution of the monasteries. The war memorial can clearly be seen in front of the tower.

Remembrance Sunday Service at St Edburg's Church, 11 November 1928. Bicester's historic links with all the services makes this an annual date of special significance.

Cottage and barn behind the church in what is now Old Place Yard. Notice the fine example of the thatcher's craft. The grassed area in front of the building is now the site of Bicester Library. The cottage and barn have long since disappeared to make way for a road and car parking.

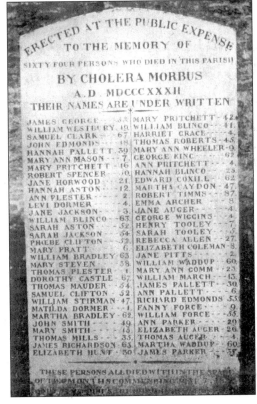

The 'Cholera Stone' situated in St Edburg's churchyard next to the entrance to Bicester Town Cemetery. This stone commemorates the death of sixty-four people in the town, when Asiatic Cholera reached the district in June 1832. The death rate in Bicester was higher in proportion to population than in any other town in England. The victims were buried in separate graves on the south side of the churchyard, near to where the stone was originally located.

ERECTED AT THE PUBLIC EXPENSE
TO THE MEMORY OF
SIXTY FOUR PERSONS WHO DIED IN THIS PARISH

BY CHOLERA MORBUS
A.D. MDCCCXXXII
THEIR NAMES ARE UNDER WRITTEN

JAMES GEORGE	53	MARY PRITCHETT	42
WILLIAM WESTBURY	19	WILLIAM BLINCO	41
SAMUEL CLARK	67	HARRIET GRACE	4
JOHN EDMONDS	48	THOMAS ROBERTS	45
HANNAH PALLETT	39	MARY ANN WHEELER	9
MARY ANN MASON	7	GEORGE KINC	62
MARY PRITCHETT	46	ANN PRITCHETT	4
ROBERT SPENCER	50	HANNAH BLINCO	25
JANE HORWOOD	21	EDWARD COXILL	62
HANNAH ASTON	12	MARTHA CAYDON	47
ANN PLESTER	2	ROBERT TIMMS	87
LEVI DORMER	4	EMMA ARCHER	8
JANE JACKSON	3	JANE AUGER	4
WILLIAM BLINCO	63	GEORGE WIGGINS	4
SARAH ASTON	52	HENRY TOOLEY	7
SARAH JACKSON	54	SARAH TOOLEY	5
PHŒBE CLIFTON	52	REBECCA ALLEN	27
MARY PRATT	6	ELIZABETH COLEMAN	8
WILLIAM BRADLEY	65	JANE PITTS	2
MARY STEVEN	58	WILLIAM WADDUP	60
THOMAS PLESTER	4	MARY ANN COMM	23
DOROTHY CASTLE	67	WILLIAM MARCH	43
THOMAS MAUDER	54	JAMES PALLETT	39
SAMUEL CLIFTON	52	ANN PALLETT	6
WILLIAM STIRMAN	47	RICHARD EDMONDS	55
MATILDA DORMER	4	FANNY FORCE	9
MARTHA BRADLEY	62	WILLIAM FORCE	55
JOHN SMITH	49	ANN PARKER	29
MARY SMITH	13	ELIZABETH AUGER	26
THOMAS MILLS	35	THOMAS AUGER	4
JAMES RICHARDSON	65	MARTHA WADDUP	60
ELIZABETH HUNT	50	JAMES PARKER	37

THESE PERSONS ALL DIED WITHIN THE SPACE
OF TWO MONTHS COMMENCING IN

Church Street, next to the church looking west, *c*. 1900. The children stand reading a notice on the doors to the old police station and courthouse, built in 1837. After many years of neglect, it has now been converted into two private houses.

'Domino School' at the Police Social Club *c*. 1953 in a room above the old Police Station in Church Street. A young Peter Judd (aged fifteen) worked behind the bar and received two pints of beer per session in payment. His father, retired policemen Stan Judd, is seated on the left. The other players are, from left to right: George Goble (local grocer), Harris Morgan (photographer), Jim Jones (Detective Constable), Fred Ferris (Sergeant).

Two

The Causeway and South of Market Square

The Causeway looking west towards the church. Notice the overhang on the very old building on the right, 8 The Causeway, now an Indian restaurant. The first building on the left was Mr Smith's second bakery shop. The scene looks much the same today.

Mr E. Smith (right) and his son Mr W. E. Smith (left), outside their bakery shop in The Causeway, c. 1900. In the background is a brewery wagon, probably having made a delivery to the Rose and Crown that can be seen behind it. Alternatively, it may have come from Shillingford's brewery, which was behind the buildings on the left.

Looking west along the Causeway towards the church, c. 1935. The gates on the right led to Bonner's Yard. The Prince of Wales (later Edward VIII) was a frequent visitor to the stables here, from where he rode out with the Bicester Hunt.

Bicester Army Cadets parade led by Sgt Mick Smith, 1952. The policeman is Sgt Stan Judd. The ground behind the wall was developed and became Bicester's Roman Catholic church, opened in 1963.

The Causeway, c. 1960 – a very tight squeeze for this transporter, moving a plane fuselage one winter's afternoon. No-one now remembers just why it was passing through the town.

The Causeway looking west, 18 October 1939. Notice the gas mask being carried by the young man at the front. The gate on the right leads to the swimming pool, built on land owned by Bicester Urban District Council.

Grand opening of the open-air pool, June 1933. The building of the pool was a project to create work for the unemployed.

The lucky ones jump in on the first day, June 1933. A draw had been made to select the first to take the plunge and 'christen' the new pool.

At the opening, June 1933 – swimming fashions of the day. How things change!

Water Lane, renamed Chapel Street. This was the old main road into the town from the London direction. It was liable to flooding and extremely muddy. Notice the high causeway built to the left of the roadway. The first house on the left became the manse for the Congregational Chapel, which was built further up the road on the right. Today the chapel building is home to a snooker club and the manse is a private house.

Roadworks in Chapel Street in the early part of the twentieth century. The view today is very different many of the buildings having disappeared. The building at the far end of the street is the Rose and Crown, demolished to make way for Manorsfield Road.

Priory Road – at the far end is Marlborough Terrace which has two inscribed dates, 1903 and 1905. Marlborough Villas, built by George Layton and named after the Duke of Marlborough of Blenheim Palace, Woodstock, is dated 1907. The terrace nearest the camera has no date stone, but appears to have been built in the same period.

St Edburg's Hall, built in 1882. The Revd Blackburn-Kane had only been in Bicester a few months when he set out on his crusade to build a Parochial Hall for the town. Within a year and £1,000 pounds later, St Edburg's Hall was built on land donated by auctioneer Mr Jona Paxton. The man in this scene, around 1885, is unknown.

Rose Cottage, Bicester.

Picture postcard of Rose Cottage, London Road. The photograph of St Edburg's Hall was taken from the gate of this property. Notice the formal garden of this substantial town residence. In August 1905, when General Booth, founder of the Salvation Army, visited the town (see p. 51) he was entertained to tea at this house by the owner Mrs Palmer.

London Road looking north towards the town centre *c.* 1953. To the left, on the corner of Priory Road is the Regal Cinema, opened in 1934. The house on the right is the 'Hermitage'. Beyond this building, in a private garden, is the old town lock-up where prisoners were kept before being taken to jail.

Staff on the steps of the Regal Cinema *c.* 1945. From left to right, back row: Dennis Marriott, Frank Brittain, Ken East, Bill Lissimer, Gordon Jones. Middle row: Arthur Winfield, Doreen Ward, 'Dinky' Pearce, Cynthia Blowfield, Sylvia Massey, Joe Price. Front row: Elsie Dancer, Betty Pickup, Fred Smith (manager), Joyce Marriot, 'Malc' Campbell.

Properties at the junction of the London and Launton Roads after a snowstorm, 26 April 190?
The man in the centre is clearing snow from outside Timberlake's shop. George Timberlake wa
a cooper, umbrella repairer, cutler, ironmonger and dealer in paraffin.

Looking east along the Launton Road
around 1890, from its present day
junction with Victoria Road. Behind
the wall on the right is the stable
block of Garth House. The Council
developed the left-hand side of the
road for housing just after the Second
World War. Garth House is now hom
to Bicester Town Council and the
grounds are a public park.

Three

Market Square

The Square, 14 October 1925. In the centre is the 'Hedges Block' with a pedestrian passageway to the right and a narrow vehicular passage on the left. An old postcard of the same view describes the building with the small 'tower' on the left as the 'Council Chamber and Masonic Rooms'. No documentary evidence can be found to support this.

London Road & Market Square, Bicester

East side of London Road and Market Square on a postcard marked 'Bicester 7pm, 18 July 1916'. Note the Dijon car, which belonged to Dr Hendricks. The message on the reverse read 'Dear Lizzie I hope you and family are well You will see I am at Ada's came last Friday week think of stopping 2 more weeks I am feeling much better than I were A and I are well how your husband getting about the war will he have to go I wish it were over did you get to see your mother and did you get that 'posay' (sic) I sent I was pleased to hear from your Brother Charli love to all from Aunt Emma'. Notice the lack of punctuation.

A portrait of Dr Hendricks with his dog. This photograph was sent to a friend as a Christmas present. He was a kind, charitable man, well loved by the people of the town. It is reputed that he never sent out a bill, which was helpful to poorer folk who otherwise would have received no medical care.

The caption on the card, 'Bicester – Market Hill and Station Road', is interesting. Today the addresses of these buildings are Market Square and London Road. Pankhurst, who produced this card, was a local publisher and therefore some credence must be given to the street names on it. The workmen are probably laying water pipes, which were installed in the town in 1905.

The Hunt outside the King's Arms Hotel c. 1851. Notice the policeman wearing the high top hat in the centre behind the hounds. This is probably the traditional Boxing Day meet. The banner on the wall of the hotel is wishing them success.

Three public houses in one scene *c.* 1900. The King's Arms Hotel is in the foreground, the Nag's Head with the two bay windows further along, and the King's Head in the background. This view is little changed today.

Mr John Dearn, licensee of the King's Head and the proprietor of Dearn's Garage, which was next door in what was formerly the Nag's Head public house. He was a well-known local character in the years between the wars and had the first charabanc in the town.

The 'Hedges Block' c. 1960. The block included Hedges' drapery and outfitter. On the other side were the Covent Garden Fruit Stores (which also sold wool) and a café. The narrow road- passage to the left of the Hedges Block was the main vehicular route through the town. As the size of vehicles increased it became inadequate (see p. 37).

Scaffolding on a building on 'the island' of Market Square c. 1950. Of note is the exposed timber frame and windows. The renovated building can be seen (far left) in the picture above.

A fancy dress line-up in front of Claremont House during the Coronation celebrations in 1911. The 'caveman' to the right of centre is Mr Morley Wilfred Smith and to the left of him, dressed as 'night and day', is Marjorie Smith. The pillared doorway on the right has disappeared, but the entrance survives as the access to Dean's Court shops.

A crowd gathers at the back of the 'Hedges Block' to look at the floods at the southern end of Sheep Street, 4 July 1915. The narrow foot passage can be seen to the left side of the buildings, and the vehicular passage to the right.

A lorry crashes into the side of the 'Hedges Block', 30 March 1962. A local paper reported that an army lorry travelling to Bicester Garrison failed to negotiate the narrow bottleneck at the southern end of Sheep Street and caused damage to the wool shop on the corner. Mrs Hunt can be seen discussing the situation with an army driver and a local policeman. The buildings were demolished in 1963 in order to ease traffic congestion through the town.

Market Square looking west towards The Causeway. The horse and cart stand outside Bourto the Carrier's premises, 29 Market Square. On the other side are the Rose and Crown and further along, Bridge House. Both properties were demolished to make way for Manorsfiel Road and the National Westminster Bank building.

The Fountain, Market Square c. 1930. Although called a fountain, it was actually three drinking troughs in the shape of a cloverleaf. As well as troughs for animals, it had three push-button spouts for humans.

Looking towards 'the island' of the Market Square c. 1930. The third building on the right was a shop run by Miss Scrivener. It is said that during the war years, it was like going into a Dickensian shop. Miss Scrivener, so the story goes, would use a trap door in the floor to fetch items from a storeroom below, causing small children to wonder if she had disappeared forever!

The 'funnel' shape of the Market Square can be seen in this aerial photograph taken between the wars. To the extreme left (centre), behind the King's Head, the lighter rectangular shape of the town's bowling green can quite clearly be seen.

A busy Market Square on the day of the Wool Fair in 1905. Notice the variety of Oxfordshire wagons and other carts. The two small boys wearing black armbands at the bottom of the picture may be in mourning. The second building on the right was occupied by the *Bicester Herald,* founded by George Hewiett in 1855.

The Coronation celebrations 1911. The Market Square is well decorated with both Union and St George's flags. Notice the photographer with the tripod camera on the right, who is using the low roof of the Cross Keys Inn as a vantage point. The ladies' hats and children in bonnets make careful study of this scene rewarding.

Staff outside H. C. Jagger's 'Veterinary Shoeing Forge', 17 Market Square. Notice the grill at the bottom of the building behind the men on the right, an indication of the large cellars that existed underneath these old buildings. Just noticeable is the cobbled path from the street to the yard for the horses.

Harris Morgan & Son's photographers shop, 18 Market Square. The cobbled path can still be seen leading from the street to the yard of the building next door.

Staff outside the Post Office, 10 Market Square (now Sketchley Cleaners), *c.* 1888. The sign above the door says 'Money Order Office and Post Office Savings Bank'. Notice on the right the mailbags, which are printed with the names of dispatching and receiving towns. The large baskets were probably brought out into the street especially for the occasion. Of particular note is the small boy at the front (left) and the impressive delivery bicycle. The young woman standing behind the men in the centre of the picture, is Miss French. She held the distinction of being the first woman in Oxfordshire to qualify for Post Office service in 1887.

Clearing the Market Square after Empire Shopping Week celebrations, 20-25 July 1931. The men, from left to right are: -?-, Syd Grimes (draper) on the lorry, Mr Plant (?), Jack Fisher (electrician), Harry Stillgoe (foreman, Wessex Electric), H. T. Smith (town surveyor, Urban District Council), Ted Charles (manager, Wessex Electric). On the edge of the picture with a broom is Morley Smith (confectioner and baker).

Traditional ox roast on the Market Square, 4 November 1933. Mrs Violet Gilbey of Slade Farm is seen here about to taste the first cut, a traditional way to start the celebrations.

A wet day for the traditional Boxing Day meet of the Hunt, Christmas 1962.

Battle of Britain Parade, 1962. The parade makes its way from the church, along The Causeway and into the Market Square. The salute is taken between two aircraft. At the very bottom is a Chipmunk T.10 of the Oxford University Air Squadron. More prominent is an LF.16 Spitfire, which stood at the gate of RAF Bicester.

Four

Sheep Street

Looking north up Sheep Street, a view on a postcard, *c.* 1920.

The 'George Corner' looking west into the Market Square. *c.* 1910. On the right-hand corner is the George Hotel which was demolished to make way for the Midland Bank, No. 1 Sheep Street. Further along is the Post Office (see p. 42). On the opposite corner is the end building of 'the island' with an interesting balcony roof on which another storey of the building once stood.

Bicester, Oxon.

IMPORTANT ANNUAL SALE

OF HIGH-CLASS

WINES.

MESSRS.

JONAS PAXTON, SON, & CASTLE

Have received instructions from Messrs. JAMES PETTIT & COMPANY,

To Sell by Auction,

AT THE GEORGE INN, BICESTER,

On *FRIDAY, DECEMBER* 15th, 1876,

AT TWO FOR THREE O'CLOCK,

100 DOZ. SHERRY,

120 DOZEN OF PORT,

30 Doz. Champagne, 20 Doz. Claret.

Samples of the Wines will be produced at the time of Sale.

Catalogues may be obtained of Messrs. James Pettit and Company, Aylesbury, Leighton Buzzard, and 71, Borough High Street, London; or of the Auctioneers, Bicester.

Robert Gibbs, Printer, Bourbon-Street, Aylesbury.

A wine sale catalogue. The event, which took place at the George Inn (Hotel), comprised 270 lots. An extract from the catalogue reads: 'Lot 191. One dozen 1872 Port. This wine has immense body and flavour, with grand character, and is strongly recommended for laying down. Sealed black.' This was followed with twenty-nine identical lots.

The 'George Corner', 1930s, after the George Hotel had been demolished and the Midland Bank had taken its place. The furniture shop on the opposite corner was owned by George Harris. Notice the furniture on display on the pavement. The policeman in the middle of the road is presumably on traffic duty!

This postcard of Sheep Street, postmarked 7.15p.m. 23 July 1909, captures life in a small market town at the turn of the century. It was sent to Mrs Garbet of Buxton, Derbyshire, by Dorothy Deacon from Hilton Booteries, Market Hill. The card reads: 'Dear Grandma. We have not forgot you. It was our Sunday School treat yesterday (Thursday) we went to Oddington in brakes. Mary had a silk ribbon to go across her hair for a prize. I didn't go in a race. Arthur had a bat. I will now close with love and kisses from all to all. xxxxxxxx Dorothy Deacon xxxx'.

Street market, *c.* 1908. Of interest is the printed caption on the back of this postcard. It reads: 'Bicester Market – the continuance of the fortnightly sales in Bicester streets has been prohibited by the Board of Agriculture after Sept. 1 next. The question now is: Will the electors authorise the Urban Council to provide a market at about £2,000 or let the Auctioneers provide their own sale yard? A poll is to be taken on the subject.' Despite the prohibition, markets still operated after this date. The market eventually moved to the present Victoria Road site in 1910. Notice on the right, the items from Palmer Brothers Ironmongers adding to the street scene.

The last Cattle Market. The two groups make an interesting contrast. The herd of cattle on the right stands quietly, while on the left next to the sheep pens a group of girls in bonnets take in the scene. The large building in the centre of the top row, now demolished, is the Crown Hotel.

Palmer Brothers Ironmongers *c.* 1905. The business later became Palmer & Ashmore and then Ashmore & Son. The building was destroyed by fire and replaced by the present Ashmore premises.

Two hounds go their own way (extreme right) as the Bicester Hunt moves along Sheep Street in 1953. Lloyds Bank (10 Sheep Street) and Ashmore & Son (6-8 Sheep Street) are still there today.

A coach waits outside Ashmore's and the White Hart public house to take members of the Sunshine Club on holiday, sometime during the 1950s.

Sheep Street looking south, *c.* 1885, shows the unbroken line of posts used for tethering cattle on market days.

Camels follow elephants in a circus parade c. 1900. The Crown Hotel can be seen dominating the left-hand side of the picture.

Another important visitor outside the Crown Hotel, August 1905. General William Booth, founder of the Salvation Army, visited Bicester to address a meeting in the Corn Exchange, which was situated behind the Crown Hotel.

Boy's Brigade parade *c.* 1908. The large gateway on the left led to the Corn Exchange behind the Crown Hotel. This became the Crown Cinema in 1921 and after a fire in 1943 was renovated into a dance hall. This is now the site of the Crown Walk shopping precinct. The building with the high arched gateway further along the street was the International Stores.

Staff outside 21 Sheep Street, the International Stores, *c.* 1919. Stores such as this were the beginning of today's supermarkets. Groups of shops bought food in bulk so that they could keep prices down. Much of the food was imported. The advertising poster in the window reads: 'Economy – Quality also'.

Mr Morley Smith stands outside the family shop, 23 Sheep Street, with members of the scout troupe. The sale, to raise money for the Red Cross, is believed to have been held in around 1915. The girl on the extreme left is Cicely Smith who died in the flu epidemic of 1918. The British Heart Foundation charity shop now occupies this building. The doors to the right have now been incorporated into the display windows of the adjoining property, 25 Sheep Street.

Alf Evans opened his outfitters business at Nos. 29 and 31 Sheep Street in 1902. Here he can be seen to the right of the archway outside 31 Sheep Street in 1906. Through the archway today is a small parade of shops named Evans Yard.

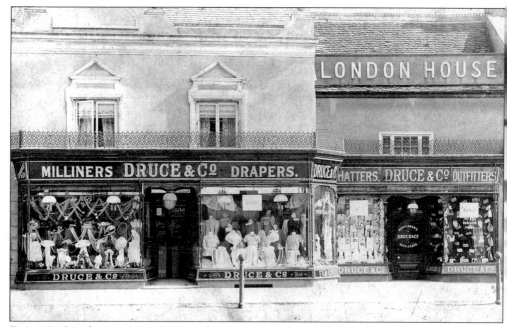

Druce & Co. drapers, Nos. 22 (London House) and 24 Sheep Street. Notice the elaborate window display of a sort very seldom seen today. The shop sign showed gold lettering on a black background. The shop was extensively damaged by fire in 1916. Prior to 1900, London House was the Bear Inn, one of the principal drinking houses in the town.

Children cycle along Sheep Street accompanied by a dog, c. 1934. It looks as if the children are holding rolled-up towels and could well be making their way home from the swimming pool, which opened in The Causeway in 1933.

An ordinary day in Sheep Street, August 1930. A closer look at the sky reveals the R100 airship.

At the time of this photograph, the imposing building on the right, 49 Sheep Street, was the home of Dr Long. In the 1960s it did service as a Labour Exchange. Until recently, when renovation work removed it, the brass letterbox bearing the name 'Ministry of Labour' was still under the window to the left of the door. The building is now the town centre's Tesco supermarket.

Sheep Street looking north with North Street beyond, *c.* 1890. The buildings on the right were demolished to make way for the Methodist Church, built in 1926. Notice the man, on the pavement just before the cart, carrying two pails suspended from a yoke over his shoulders.

S. A. Stevens, pork butcher, 86 Sheep Street: showing off the Christmas produce shortly after the First World War. A young Arthur Grace, seen here on the right, later set up his own butcher's shop across the road at 53 Sheep Street.

Nos. 53-57 Sheep Street, c. 1925. The first cottage on the left was Mr Grace's butchers shop where meat was displayed in the left-hand window. It is probably Mr Grace standing in the doorway with knife in hand. Notice too, the drop-handlebar bicycle leaning against the window.

A fire in the thatch of 57 Sheep Street, 1927. Damage was also caused to 55; Mr Grace at 53 took the precaution of removing the meat from his shop. The contents of the house were removed to the front of the Methodist Church opposite. Note the crowd of young boys clinging to the railings for a better look and the fireman in brass helmet at the top of the ladder.

Stone-laying ceremony of the Wesleyan Methodist Church, 23 September 1926. The Revd Ernest D. Green lays the first stone to the memory of the late Revd Grainger Hargreaves. The small boy behind the fence in the centre of the picture is George Rose who grew up to leave the town and become an accomplished actor. To the right is the Revd Alfred Fretwell, minister of the church from 1925 to 1928.

Opening ceremony of the Methodist Church, 23 June 1927.

A scene published in the *Picture Post*, 1950.
'Wish I belonged to the Sunday School '.
The Methodist Church had been established
in this building for over twenty-two years.

A fund-raising event, *c*. 1955. The proceeds of the brick 'sale' went towards building the Sunday School halls in the garden at the rear of the church in Victoria Road.

Wesley Hall (1890-1954), formerly the United Methodist Free Church (1863-1890). Today the façade at street level has been much altered and the building is used for commercia purposes. On the left is 69 Sheep Street, R. V. Jones family grocery shop.

A scene published in the *Picture Post*, 1950. 'Town still asleep – except for the Sunday School Sid Hedges gathers the children outside Wesley Hall.

No. 69 Sheep Street decorated for the Queen's Jubilee in 1977. The building was originally built as a reading room provided by the Earl of Jersey.

Peter Judd and his son discover a well during building work behind their shop, R. V. Jones, 69 Sheep Street, 1992. The well, on land that was once Providence Farm, was found intact with a perfect clay lining.

Inside a family grocers shop during filming for a Heinz Company training film, c. 1986. The shop was chosen because of its authentic old style grocer's interior. Peter Judd, who can be seen behind the counter retained the interior of the shop after taking over the business from his uncle R. V. Jones.

The film crew brings a touch of Pinewood Studios to the quiet market town.

Five
Top of the Town

BUCKINGHAM RD BICESTER.

postcard from sometime after the railway was built over Buckingham Road in 1906. The
ater pump has since been replaced by a road sign at this busy junction. Before the houses on
e right were built, it really was 'Top o' the Town'.

The Crockwell area of the town at the corner of St John's Street and Sheep Street. Th
building on the left was the Star public house. The buildings were demolished in 1967 to mak
way for car parking.

Further west along St John's Street, a row of cottages which have now disappeared. A row
houses stands there now, further back from the road.

Crockwell School, fondly remembered as the 'little school', opened in 1868 and remained in use until 20 July 1972. The school bell hung in the gable under the weathervane. A child who was considered to have behaved well had the daily privilege of ringing the bell. A cellar under the front of the building was used for the storage of coal and coke to fuel the stoves.

Teacher and pupils of Crockwell School, c. 1909.

Buckingham Road, looking north, before the railway embankment and bridge were built i 1906.

Buckingham Road, Bicester.

Buckingham Road looking south towards 'Top o' the Town', *c.* 1930.

East side of North Street, January 1937. The road became one way (travelling south) in 1944. Notice the street lamp on the left. The streets of Bicester were first lit by gas in 1845. By the time of this picture the town was well serviced by electricity.

North Street looking south towards Sheep Street, January 1937. Notice the circular Bicester sign on the wall of the cottage on the left. The row of cottages on the right was demolished in the late 1970s to make way for a block of flats.

North Street looking north. In the previous century the road was gated at this point and a toll had to be paid in order to proceed. Notice the sign above the door on the building on the right. It reads: 'Accommodation for cyclists – lodgings'.

Further up North Street towards 'Top o' the Town'. The buildings on the left are much the same today, although those on the right have been replaced by modern housing.

Six
People and
Entertainment

The cast of a Bicester amateur dramatic group's production of *Princess Ju-Ju*, 1914.

County School's production of Gilbert and Sullivan's *Iolanthe* in 1937. Standing on the right the producer Mr J. N. Davies, who was also the French master and boys' P.E. master. Standing on the left is the pianist Mr Parry. The cast members are from left to right, back row: K.C. Daniels, H. Ayers, N. Goss, K. Elias, F. Long, H. Orchard, D.J. Curtis, R. Herring, F.V. Vaughan, V. Redfern. Second row (standing): Esme Scarrott, B. Cambray, S. Mood, D. Carter, L. Wickson, G.T. James, A.W. Scarrott, G. Tompkin, Roger Smith, F.A. Jenkin, Frances Mould (present member of the Bicester Local History Society). Third row (seated): Jean Hoddinot, Hilda Morpeth, Ellen Denny, Kathleen Ferriman, Kathleen Moss, Daphne Hillier, Margaret Rogers, Olive Booth, Margaret Reeves, Cynthia Brain, Evelyn Clayton. Front row: Grace Orchard, Irene Addison, Joan Shurmer, Iris Bachelor, Pansy Alderman, Joyce Dickens, Patricia Whipp, Joyce Bailey.

ocial Club amateur dramatic production of *She Stoops to Conquer*, December 1927. In this rinking scene, several well-known Bicester characters can be seen. Seated fourth from the left nd raising a tankard is Reg Grimes, men's outfitter. Also standing is Bert Freeman, cobbler of 1e Causeway. Seated at the end of the table in tailcoat holding a riding crop, and having his ankard filled, is Tom Hudson JP.

'roduction of *Journey's End*, December 1933. Actors from left to right, standing, are: -?-, Mr /hetton, Reg Grimes (men's outfitter), Mr Harcourt Smith (builder), -?-, -?-, Bert Freeman. eated: Tom Dean (ironmonger), Fred Waine (butcher), James Davies (schoolmaster), Mr libring (pharmacist), Tom Hudson (tobacconist), Mr F. Smith. The boy seated on the floor is red Pittuck.

Bicester Methodist Sunday School cast in a production of *Robert Raikes*, 1931. From left t
right, standing: Nellie Alley, Sid Hedges, Rose Alley, Frank Hillsdon, Gilbert Alley, Jac
Richardson, Charlie Rawlings, George Hedges. Seated: Maud Alley, Revd Harold Garn¢
(Minister 1929-1932), Joe Leach, Winnie Plant. Sitting on the ground: Pansy Barney, Glad
Whetton.

Methodist Church production of *Cinderella*, 1953. From left to right, standing: Michael Trinder (Lord Chancellor), Jacqueline Bignall (Baroness), Jennifer Trinder (Marcella), Jill Woodhouse (Prince Charming), Sid Hedges (Author), Joan Neal (Fairy Godmother), Sylvia Barnes (Gushmush), Morag Stuart (Fairy), Ann Borrow (Fairy), Mrs Foster (Costumes - Minister's Wife). Seated: Morfa Hughes (Page), Ann Woodman (Cinderella), Penny Bignall (Pixie), Jennifer Box (Fairy).

A concert party pose for the camera, c. 1920. Three of the party are: D. F. Harris (top left), Miss Dealey (centre) and Miss Mountain (bottom right). Sid Hedges, in his book *Bicester Wuz a Little Town*, recalls that in 1910 the predecessor of the concert party was the 'Orpheus Orchestra' conducted by Will Grimsley. Will was tragically killed during the First World War, but the music played on afterwards without him.

A scene published in the *Picture Post*, 1950, 'Like this, Jill, explains S.G.'. Sid Hedges takes the musicians through their paces. The Red Rhythmics harmonica band was formed in 1935 as a Sunday School band. By 1945 it had appeared at the Royal Albert Hall. When the band closed down in 1956, it had also appeared on television, gaining prestige for the Sunday School and the town.

Bicester Methodist Sunday School Red Rhythmics Band outside the Royal Albert Hall, 1945. The name derived from their scarlet berets and ties. Standing on the extreme left is Sid Hedges (Conductor). Other band members are, from left to right, back row: Wilf Smith, Tony Hedges, Cyril Perry, Joan Hoare, Dorcas Leach, Mary Crawford, Betty Baughhan. Front row: Norman Coward, Madeleine Hillsdon, Michael Brunt, Derek West, Les Blackman.

Seven
People, School and Sport

Bicester County School on the tennis court *c.* 1928. Mr John Howson, the first headmaster, sits three places to the right of the centre line. The school opened in 1924.

Bicester Methodist Church Sunday School anniversary, 1961. Many of the children are wearing special anniversary buttonholes. The guest minister on the left of the picture is the Revd Arthur Valle, minister of the church (1954-1959).

Although the children in this schoolroom photograph are unknown, it shows quite clearly the regimentation of the classroom in the early part of the twentieth century.

Bicester County School hockey team, 1948. From left to right, back row: Ann Leach, Margaret
Bridges, Barbara Tebbetts, Shirley Trowbridge, Pat Crawford, Eileen Weatherall, Miss Kerse.
Middle row: Joyce Murray, Marion Simms, Pat Taylor. Front row: Joyce Taylor, Gwen Barney,
June Barker.

A Bicester County School rugby team *c.* 1927. The boy sitting on the ground on the left is Tom Harris. Tom lived his whole life in the town and left a collection of photographs, many of which appear in this book.

A Bicester County School cricket team, *c.* 1929. Tom Harris is seated on the right in the front row. A few of the other boys can also be recognized from the rugby team picture. This photograph was taken in the garden between the school and the courtyard stable block. The garden is now the location of the Bicester Day Centre.

Bicester County School rugby players, 1925/26. Standing on the right is Mr E. T. Clothier, maths master, who became Headmaster on the retirement of Mr J. Howson in 1940.

St Edburg's School football team, 1949/50. From left to right, back row: Allan Offord, Eric Bourton, ? Curtis, T. Smith, ? Woodley, P. Whitmore, Pete Kelly, B. Joins, Ray Grimes, Tim Scarrott. Seated: Tudor Jones (sports master), Maurice Massey, D. Barker, Pat Smith, D. Roberts, Ted Shaw, Mr Price (Headmaster)

79

Bicester Methodist Sunday School football team, winners of the Hedges Cup 1959. From left to right, back row: Les Smith, Blanco Babic, John Russell, Sid Hedges, Nigel Grace, Colin Patience, Charlie Rawlings. Front row: -?-, Colin McGarry, Vic Smith, John Hughes, Tony Bracewell, David Churnside, Danny McGarry, Malcolm Sawyer, Brian Stockford.

Headmaster of St Edburg's Church School, Mr William Piggott, kicks off at the official opening of Bicester Sports Ground in 1923. The ground was formerly called Barn Piece.

The winning team of the Chipping Norton Hospital Cup, 18 April 1925. Bicester won 2-1. The players are, from left to right, back row: H. Dean, C. Cousins, -?-, A. Simons (with the cup), J. Tebby, W. Price. Front row: G. Adams, B. Haynes, -?-, T. Simons, -?-.

The spectators celebrate Bicester's first goal on their way to defeating Banbury Stones Athletic 3-1. The back of the photograph is inscribed: 'Thus gaining the Championship of the Oxon Senior League on 3 May 1928'.

Bicester Football Team, Senior League winners 1928. From left to right, back row: J. Hollis (official), J. Tebby, A. Simons, P. Ward, J. Simons, T. Simons, L. Barker, C. Harris, G. Penn (official). Front row: W. Price, -?-, -?- (mascot), B. Haynes, H. Dean.

The successful Rifle Club shows off its trophies, 1930s. Seated on the left is Mr Sibring (pharmacist). Seated on the right is Mr T. J. Mountain (chemist) who, despite having only one eye, was good enough to shoot at Bisley. The other men are, from left to right: Ernest Ward (who only had one arm!), George Penn (who only had one eye!), Tom Hearne, Jack Ansell, Harold Weatherbee, Harris Morgan, Len Bowman, Harcourt Smith, Norman James, Mr Harris, ...es Booker, -?-, Reg Grimes. The small boy behind the table is Mick Morgan, who grew up to ...ake over his father's photography business.

Superintendent Fairbrother sits proudly with trophies won by the Bicester Police tug-of-war team, c. 1920. The photograph was taken in the yard of the old Police Station in Church Street. Behind the yard wall is milkman Dagley's field where the tug-of-war took place.

Peter Harvey Judd, aged one year old, in 1930. The son of PC Stan Judd, he is pictured here trying out the scales at a tug-of-war competition. Stan pulled for both the Bicester and County Division teams.

The success of the Bicester men is evident in this photograph of the Oxford County Division team in 1931. The Bicester members are first and second left, PC Stan Judd and Bill Hermon. Fourth and fifth from the left are PC Scroggs and PC Allnutt.

Stan Judd in the yard of the Angel public house, 102 Sheep Street, where he was landlord after his retirement from the Bicester Police Force in 1953. Stan commented one day 'they will carry me out of this pub feet first', and they did!

Bicester B.C.

Nov. 1-19

Members of the Bicester Bowls Club, 1 November 1913. The Bowls Club met on land behind the King's Head (see aerial photograph on p. 39) before moving across the road to the present Town Council-owned site next to Garth Park.

Eight
People and Events

Bicester Boys' Brigade, *c.* 1907. Standing second from the right is R.V. Jones, born in 1896. He later became a grocer at 69 Sheep Street.

Drum and Fife Band, an early photograph thought to have been taken outside Bicester House

YMCA Band outside 16 Market Square, 1912. Behind the bass drum is 'Nigger' Aldridge who was an assistant stoker on the town's fire engine, hence, perhaps, his nickname.

Red Cross nurses (26th Detachment) outside St Edburg's Hall in London Road, 1927.

Bicester ex-Navy reunion, Christmas 1948. This was the beginning of the Bicester Royal Navy Association. Peter Judd, who made this photograph available, is sitting second from the left.

A wedding group from 1909. Of particular note are the splendid hats, worn by the ladies. The marriage of Maurice John Benjafield (24) bachelor, grocer's assistant of 16 Rowley Road, Reading, to Edith Evans (24) spinster, of Sheep Street, Bicester was recorded on 3 August 1909. The witnesses were Edith's father, John Wesley Evans (grocer), brother John Henry Evans, sister Florence Louisa Evans and Edith Mary Jackson. The names that have been handed down through time for this wedding group, are from left to right, back row: Maud Archer, Albert Evans, -?-, Jack Scott, Tim Clarke, Percy Evans. Middle row: Harry Jackson, Ethel Branagan, William Grimsley, Nell Harris, Harry Evans, Nell Jackson, Tom Evans, -?-, Betty Evans. Front row: Alf Evans, -?-, Floss Evans, Maurice Benjafield, Edie Benjafield (née Evans), -?-, John Wesley Evans. The woman holding the child is believed to be Nellie Evans (wife of Alf Evans). The child is probably their daughter Nellie May Evans. The Evans family was an important shopkeeping family in the town (see p. 53).

A Red Cross stall outside the White Hart, 4 Sheep Street, c. 1916. The women of Bicester stand alongside Belgian refugees. Notice the boy on the right in sailor's uniform.

A First World War picture of a fancy dress event. Seated (centre) is Evadia Viola Jones who became Mrs Stan Judd.

A New Year's Eve party at the Bicester Social Club, 31 December 1928. The days when funny glasses and a paper hat were all that was required for a good time to be had by all!

A much grander affair a year later. New Year's Eve, 31 December 1929. Christmas decorations, lanterns and paper hats are very much in evidence.

scene published in the *Picture Post*,
950. 'End of the Youth Club evening'
the forerunner of today's disco!

scene published in the *Picture Post*, 1950. 'Club canteen is open'. The Methodist Youth Club
et in the Wesley Hall in Sheep Street (see p. 60).

Methodist Church Sunday School staff in the garden behind the church on Victoria Ro?
1944. Behind the trees on the left are the old Salvation Army rooms. The people in th
wartime scene are, from left to right, back row: Norman Coward, Jack Bentley, Les Blackma
Reg Plum, Myra Plant, Jerry Larrabie, Billy Ally, Cyril Perry, Chris Luckin, Michael Brun
Middle row: Hetty McCabe, Mrs Compton, Frank Wilkins, Maud Titchner, Percy Brunt, S
Hedges, Mary Hedges, Hylda Sawyer, Les Smith, Betty Smith. Front row: Mary Burgess, Ma
Coward, Joan Hoare, Betty Baughan, Madelaine Hillsdon, Dorcas Leach.

Methodist Church Sunday School staff in the front garden of the church, Sheep Street, 196
From left to right, back row: Peggy Joyce, Ann Buttery, Sylvia Barnes, Sally Piper, Moll
Buttery, Charlie Jones, Jennifer Box, Raymond North, Mary Willett, Florence Yule. Midd
row: Frank Wilkins, Betty Smith, Ruth Stokes, Hylda Sawyer, Ernest Goodridge, Sid Hedge
Mary Hedges, Myra Plant, Gladys Haggerty, Les Blackman. Front row: Christine Your
Doreen Clifton, Ruth Jones, Malcolm Sawyer, Walter Devlin, Ralph Thomas.

r Prentice, coal and coke merchant, with horse and cart, sometime between the wars. The
mily is still in business today – but not using this type of transport!

rentice's, coal merchants loading horse-drawn carts direct from the railway wagons in the
MS yard off London Road. The family firm still works this yard today.

Empire Shopping Week opening ceremony in the Market Square, 20 July 1931. In the centre
the picture is Nellie Hawtin as Britannia. Sitting on the platform, holding flowers, is Mrs Ruc
Keene of Bignell (see p. 126) who performed the opening ceremony. The week was organised
the Bicester and District Chamber of Commerce to encourage more use of British and Empi
goods.

Tom Hudson, Chairman of the Chamber of Commerce Executive Committee, leads the Empi
Shopping Week Fancy Dress Parade dressed as a hussar. The Marsh Gibbon Band close
follows him through the Market Square.

The end of the Shopping Week parade moves along Sheep Street. The entrance to the cinema behind the Crown Hotel can be seen on the extreme left. The old wooden fire pump, which is still hidden away somewhere in the town today, is transported by horse and cart. It is believed that the cart belonged to coalman Arthur Harris. Notice the fireman in brass helmet riding up front.

A fire engine in the parade entering the Market Square from Chapel Street. It is thought that the firemen in the front are the driver, 'Nigger' Aldridge (see p. 88), H. T. Smith seated next to him, and Jack Hollis with an array of medals standing behind. Notice a second engine following and Arthur Harris's horse and cart just behind.

The 'Good Ship Bicester' joins the Fancy Dress Parade during Empire Shopping Week, July 1931.

The children's Fancy Dress Parade pause for a photograph in Sheep Street. In the background is Mountain the chemist's shop, demolished to make way for Woolworths store.

allowfield's entry in the Shopping Week Parade. Fallowfield's was an outfitter's shop on the
Market Square and in an advertising feature in the Shopping Week souvenir booklet stated:
TOP! And SHOP at the RIGHT SHOP. Which gives discount checks on all purchases.
gents for Clark's Dry Cleaning. District Agents for Aertex.'

ndians on horseback and an Arabian Prince make an interesting scene in Sheep Street during
he Shopping Week Parade.

An ox carcass on a cart outside Midland Bank in Sheep Street, 5 November 1927. It weighed 9 stones and 4 lb. and was ready to be taken into the Market Square for roasting to raise money for the Nursing Home extension.

The crowd awaits the 'first cut' ceremony to be performed by Mrs Budget, wife of the Master Bicester Hunt. The day had started at 4.30a.m. when the fire was kindled in a specially erected brick oven. Roasting began at 6a.m. and the first cut was to be made at 11a.m. The ox-roast was one of four events in the town that day. The others were a fun fair, Guy Fawkes celebration and a football match between Bicester and Banbury Harriers.

horse fair takes advantage of the sheep fair having moved to a site on the edge of town, 5 ugust 1910. Notice that the ironmongers on the right, is now named Palmer and Ashmore. he business is still owned today by the Ashmore family.

he large annual sheep fair believed to be on land at present day Fallowfields, 5 August 1910. he embankment for the railway, which arrived in 1906, can be seen in the distance beyond he trees.

New cattle market in Victoria Road, May 1910. With prohibition of the sale of livestock o
Bicester's streets (see p. 48), a purpose-built market was provided at great cost – believed to b
around £6,000.

The cattle market, c. 1952. A very similar scene to those of 1910. The main difference being th
replacement of mature trees with cattle lorries. After a number of years of closure, the mark
finally reopened for business in 1998.

The annual Christmas Fat Stock Show on the outskirts of the town, c. 1952. Proud farmers exhibit their prized livestock.

Rogation Sunday 1959. A tractor and plough are brought into the front garden of the Methodist Church in Sheep Street, from Turney's at Weston-on-the-Green.

Bicester Sheep Fair 1962

Annual Sheep Fair, 1962. This was a major event in the farming calendar and Mr Miller, th[e] auctioneer, keeps a large crowd entertained. Notice the expanse of sheep pens and the numb[er] of lorries in the distance. The Miller family still operates the cattle market in the middle of th[e] town today.

heep Street, 23 July 1925. A violent hailstorm left the town flooded. A car succeeds here in
anoeuvring through the floodwater outside the White Hart.

or the man on the cycle, getting through the flood outside Ashmores takes a little more
concentration and effort, while the horse, travelling in the opposite direction, takes it in his
tride.

The Prince of Wales, later to be King Edward VIII, walks to a waiting car at Bicester Nort[h] railway station. He was probably visiting the town for a day's hunting.

Two large vehicles become entangled in North Street, April 1931. The road was finally made [a] one-way street in 1944.

riory Close, 1954. This is the day an RAF plane crashed into the police house belonging to ergeant Fred Ferris. On the far right, fireman Wilf Smith looks at the cockpit from where the ilot had been taken. Although no civilians were hurt, the pilot died.

Workmen remove a malt tower, January 1928. The exact location is uncertain, but it could well have been at Shillingford's brewery site in The Causeway.

Peter Judd outside 55 Sheep Street before its demolition in the late 1960s. Peter's parents moved to the house shortly after it was renovated following the 1927 fire (see p. 57), and Peter was born in the house. The town centre Tesco supermarket now occupies the site.

Nine
RAF Bicester

This is thought to be No. 118 Squadron with a Bristol F2b 'Fighter' (left) and an Avro 504K (right), *c.* 1918.

Officers and Men of C Flight, No. 100 (B) Squadron, *c. 1929*. Front row, left to right: Plt Off Stapleton, Flg Off. Pilcher, Flt Lt Drummond, Plt Off. Bucton, -?-.

The airfield looking north-west, 1935. The taxiway between the hangars disappeared when the two centre hangars were built in 1937 (see p. 113). The rail link, which ran into the stores, with a spur to the coal yard, is on the left of the picture.

No. 90 (B) Squadron, March 1938, shortly after receiving a full complement of Blenheims.

Officers, Warrant Officers and Senior Commissioned Aircrew of No. 90 (B) Squadron, c. 1937.
Note Flt Lt Heffernan in the front row in his darker RAAF uniform.

NAFFI break, 10a.m.-10.30a.m. daily, May 1938. Ground crew of No. 90 (B) Squadron havin
a well-earned tea and 'wad' (a thick sandwich) at the mobile canteen.

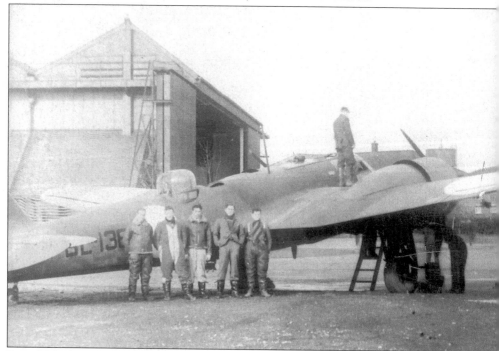

Bristol Blenheims for Finland, February 1940. The Finnish aircrew stands by a Blenheim Mk.1
before flying back to their home country.

...he airfield, 1939. Note the
...l and paint markings to
...present hedgerows in an
...tempt to camouflage the
...rfield. Two new hangers are
...place.

3ristol Blenheim Mk.1 of No. 90 (B) Squadron, 1938.

His Majesty King George VI during his visit to RAF Bicester in July 1940. The King carried o[...]
an investiture for the award of the DFC to Flt Lt Coutts-Wood. Notice that all the men, wit[...]
the exception of the King, carry service respirators.

Early Bristol Blenheim crash, 1937. The pilot escaped unhurt.

Ten

Chesterton

iew in Chesterton. 5 February 1892, 11.30am. Notice the toy horse on wheels being pulled by he small boy. The photographs in this section were found in a bound album, which was rescued om a bonfire. They give a wonderful insight into life in a small village at the end of the ineteenth century. Most of the pictures were accompanied by a caption (printed throughout iis chapter in italics) including the time, date and place.

Our Cottage, Chesterton. 9 February 1892 2.12pm. Ivy Cottage was the home of the Hughes family. In the 1891 census the household was recorded as: William M. Hughes, head, widow, aged seventy-five and living by his 'own means'; Edith E. M. Hughes, daughter, widow, aged forty-six, School Governess. George Cumberland Hughes, grandson, aged sixteen, infant; Rosamond Hughes, granddaughter, aged eight, scholar; Belinda J. Upstone, general servant – domestic, aged sixteen.

George Cumberland Hughes and cat. 20 January 1894 (Film). The identity of the photographer of this set of pictures is uncertain. It could have been George, or any other member of the family. It is interesting to note that this photograph is recorded as being taken on film. There is only one other photograph in the album with this comment.

...he front garden of Ivy Cottage.
...May 1892, 1.30pm. Grandfather
...ughes with granddaughter
...osamond Hope Hughes.

...ack garden of our house and outhouse.
...3 December 1892, 11.05am. This is
...resumably George's mother Edith
...a frosty day.

Ivy Cottage garden from the back door. 9 February 1892, 1.15pm. Rosamond in the garden doesn't look too eager to get digging! Notice the beehives at the bottom of the garden.

View on Mr Malin's Lawn. 21 December 1892, 10.30am. Rosamond is in the centre of the picture with friends.

...ridge on the Oxford Road, up stream. 13 April 1893, 3.15pm. George stands on the left; the ...her men are unknown.

...oot bridge, Oxford Road. 10 March 1892, 4.15pm. Grandfather is with a top hat and pipe. ...eorge sits on the right.

The Lawn Chesterton Lodge. c. 1894. The house is very little-changed today. It was built in 18: for Bicester banker Henry Tubb.

View in the grounds of Chesterton Lodge. 1894. The girl sitting under the tree in a summer hat presumably Rosamond.

the grounds – Chesterton Lodge. 28 February 1893, 12.40pm.

Chesterton Village, 1895. These are thought to be farm buildings on land belonging to hesterton Lodge behind the Red Cow. Notice the roof of the large glasshouse, just visible on e far left.

View from our garden gate. Christmas day, 9.30am. c. 1891. This shows the Red Cow Inn at the end of a snow-laden lane.

The Red Cow Inn. 29 July 1892, 10.45am. These may be members of the Buckle family, who ra the Inn, standing outside.

ew in Chesterton. White frost – 21 December, 10.20am. 1892. Notice the man pushing the *heelbarrow*, and the village pump on the left.

ront of the Vicarage, Chesterton. 29 December 1892, 11.10am.

Philip Tanner & pony. 15 July 1892, 11.30am. Philip lived at Manor Farm and he is pictur[ed] here on the front lawn of the farmhouse.

At Bignell. 9 March 1894, 12.30pm. Notice the girl on the left has a hoop and stick. Rosamo[nd] is standing (centre) with a pram. Another friend holds a doll.

Children's Fête. 1 May 1893, 9.20am. Notice the May garland with the pole through it in the centre of the picture. Different villages had their own traditions - another was to tie flowers to a broom handle and take your own 'May Pole' to school.

Children's Fête. 1 May 1893, 9.30am. All the children are dressed in their Sunday best.

Bignell House. 5 April 1893, 12.10pm. Facing East. Much of this grand house has disappeared
was built between 1860 and 1866 for descendants of Sir Francis Drake at a cost of £5,500.
1892 a nursery wing was added, which is all that remains today.

An unusual event. A photograph in the album without a caption. Girls can clearly be se
playing croquet on the lawn – probably of Bignell House.

...ell House. Entrance Front.
...March 1894, 2.45pm. The
...ctacular roofline is an interesting
...hitectural feature.

...nell House from the moat. 19 April 1893, 3pm.

The moat Bignell. 19 April 1893, 2.45pm. Notice Rosamond standing by the small boathouse the right.

View on the moat Bignell. 28 December 1892, 3pm. Skating on the moat just after Christm Perhaps the girls are trying out their Christmas presents.